RESCUE MISSIONS

JAMES BOW

Crabtree Publishing Company

www.crabtreebooks.com

Crabtree Publishing Company

www.crabtreebooks.com

Author: James Bow
Project editor: Tom Jackson
Designer: Lynne Lennon
Picture researcher: Sophie Mortimer
Indexer: Kay Ollerenshaw
Managing editor: Miranda Smith
Art director: Jeni Child
Design manager: David Poole
Editorial director: Lindsey Lowe
Children's publisher: Anne O'Daly
Editor: Michael Hodge
Proofreaders: Adrianna Morganelli, Crystal Sikkens
Project coordinator: Robert Walker
Production coordinator: Katherine Kantor
Font management: Mike Golka
Prepress technician: Katherine Kantor

This edition published in 2009 by
Crabtree Publishing Company.

The Brown Reference Group plc,
First Floor, 9–17 St. Albans Place,
London, N1 0NX
www.brownreference.com

Copyright © 2009 The Brown Reference Group plc

Photographs:
Alamy: Ashley Cooper: p. 11 (left); Guy Croft:
p. 10 (left); Tom Kidd: p. 4–5; Galen Rowell:
p. 18, 23 (right); tf2: p. 10 (right); Dave Willis:
p. 20 (left)
BRG: p. 8, 9 (bottom)
Corbis: Ashley Cooper: p. 18–19; Robert Maass:
p. 24–25; Reuters: p. 25 (bottom), 26, 27 (top),
28, 29; Hans Strand: p. 14 (bottom); U.S. Coast
Guard: p. 13, 14–15
RNLI: p. 15 (right), 17 (bottom), 30
Shutterstock: James B. Adson: p. 19 (bottom),
22 (left); Condor 36: p. 7 (top); Eric Gevaert:
p. 12–13; David Hancock: p. 5 (right); Todd S.
Holder: p. 6–7, 7 (bottom); JK: p. 21 (bottom);
Falk Kienas: p. 11 (right); Jason Maehl: p. 19 (top),
22 (right); Mayskyphoto: p.13 (top); Frances A.
Miller: p. 24 (bottom); John Sartin: p. 9 (top);
Carolina K. Smith: p. 27 (bottom); James Steidl:
p. 6 (bottom); Wessel du Plooy: p. 23 (left); Dr.
Morley Read: p. 20–21; Manfred Steinbach: cover;
Ingvar Tjostheim: p. 16 (left), 16 (right), 17 (top left),
17 (top right); Vasyl Yakobchuk: p. 25 (top)

Every effort has been made to trace the owners of
copyrighted material.

Library and Archives Canada Cataloguing in Publication

Bow, James, 1972-
    Rescue missions / James Bow.

(Science solves it)
Includes index.
ISBN 978-0-7787-4169-5 (bound).–ISBN 978-0-7787-4176-3 (pbk.)

1. Rescues–Juvenile literature. 2. Rescue work–Juvenile literature.
3. Fire fighters–Juvenile literature. I. Title. II. Series: Science solves
it (St. Catharines, Ont.)

HV553.B69 2008   j363.1'081   C2008-905011-8

Library of Congress Cataloging-in-Publication Data

Bow, James.
    Rescue missions / James Bow.
      p. cm. – (Science solves it)
    Includes index.
    ISBN-13: 978-0-7787-4176-3 (pbk. : alk. paper)
    ISBN-10: 0-7787-4176-1 (pbk. : alk. paper)
    ISBN-13: 978-0-7787-4169-5 (reinforced library binding : alk. paper)
    ISBN-10: 0-7787-4169-9 (reinforced library binding : alk. paper)
    1. Rescues–United States–Juvenile literature. 2. Rescue work–United States–
Juvenile literature. 3. Fire fighters–United States. I. Title. II. Series.

HV555.U6B69 2009
363.1'081–dc22
                2008033788

Crabtree Publishing Company

www.crabtreebooks.com   1-800-387-7650

**Published in Canada
Crabtree Publishing**
616 Welland Ave.
St. Catharines, ON
L2M 5V6

**Published in the United States
Crabtree Publishing**
PMB16A
350 Fifth Ave., Suite 3308
New York, NY 10118

CONTENTS

Help! 4

Chapter I
Fire and Rescue Service 6

Chapter 2
Coast Guard 12

Chapter 3
Mountain Rescue 18

Chapter 4
Terror Threat 24

Glossary 30

Further Information 31

Index 32

HELP!

When fire is spreading and flood waters are raging, the men and women of the **emergency services** are there to help.

This is a book about the men and women who risk their lives to help others. You will learn about what it takes to be a firefighter, and how the Coast Guards operate at sea. You will meet the people who swing into action when an **avalanche** strikes, and men and women who keep our cities safe from terrorist attacks.

Over the years, new tools have been invented that help save people trapped in burning houses and discover people stuck at the bottom of the ocean. Inside you learn all about robots that can dispose of bombs and helicopters that can land on water.

THE EMERGENCY SERVICES

Firefighters fight fires, police officers stop crime, and paramedics rescue the injured and sick. But they are not the only ones who save lives. The Coast Guard saves people from the ocean. Special forces deal with acts of terror, such as **hostage**-takings. And mountain rescue teams work to save people trapped on mountains and cliffs.

A rescue dog checks out a snow cave after an avalanche. Rescue dogs are trained to smell people buried in the snow.

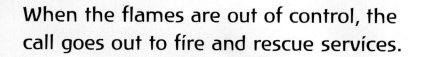

When the flames are out of control, the call goes out to fire and rescue services.

There is more to firefighting than driving the big fire truck. Firefighters do not always fight fires: their skills and equipment are useful in other areas too, from rescuing people from collapsed buildings, to saving people caught in fast-moving rivers. Whatever the situation, firefighters must work quickly. Lives depend on it.

Putting a fire out takes teamwork.

FIGHT FIRE

A fire needs **fuel** and **oxygen** to burn. Spraying the fire with water or foam blocks out the oxygen, as well making any fuel hard to burn. This helps to put out the fire and prevent it from spreading further.

CAUSES

Firefighters are also **detectives**. Once a fire is out, they need to figure out how it started. Was it an accident, or did someone set the fire on purpose?

EQUIPMENT

Firefighters are often the first to respond to a car accident. They have the equipment needed to put out fires, clean up gas and oil spills, and cut the survivors from the wreckage.

FIRE STATION

Firefighters eat and sleep at the fire station. Stations have kitchens, gyms, and bunks to sleep on. Firefighters keep their clothes washed and ready for duty. Equipment is tuned and hoses are inspected. Everything has to work perfectly.

Most stations have a pole that firefighters slide down when called to a fire. It helps firefighters get to a fire quickly. Any delay can cost lives.

DRESSED FOR ACTION

Firefighters wear protective clothing so they can work in the extreme heat near a fire. This clothing is sometimes called 'bunker gear' because firefighters once stored it under their **bunks**. Today, the gear sits ready next to the fire truck. The firefighter puts on protective pants, coat, and rubber boots.

For forest fires, helicopters scoop water out of nearby lakes to dump on the flames, and planes drop a fireproof powder. Firefighters use bulldozers to clear a "break" in the trees, or they burn a gap in the forest. This removes fuel that has not burned yet.

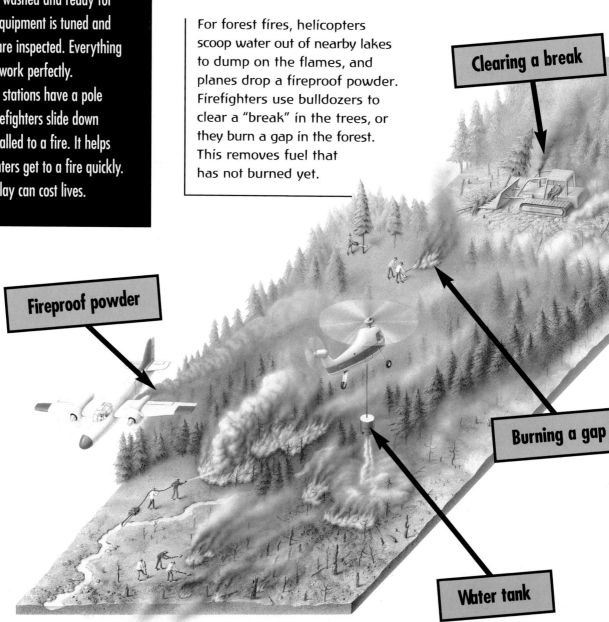

Clearing a break

Fireproof powder

Burning a gap

Water tank

A firefighter in full breathing gear. A fireproof hood covers the head under the helmet and tucks into the collar of the heavy coat.

These clothes are heat resistant and waterproof, and they also protect the firefighter from chemicals. A firefighter's helmet has a mask to protect his or her face. When it is time to go into a burning building, the firefighters carry air tanks so they do not have to breathe any poisonous smoke. Full bunker gear weighs as much as 110 pounds (50 kg). Firefighters have to stay fit so they can climb ladders while carrying their equipment and heavy hoses.

PUT THAT FIRE OUT!

It is important to find a fire early before it spreads. Smoke alarms have an electric current running through the air inside. Particles of smoke block this current, and that sets off the alarm. Now it is time to put the fire out. Sprinkler systems release huge amounts of water very quickly. They have a trigger that melts at high temperatures, opening the nozzle and shooting out water.

Some fires will not go out with water. Gasoline fires need to be put out with foam—water will make them explode! Electric fires need a powder or **carbon-dioxide fire extinguisher**.

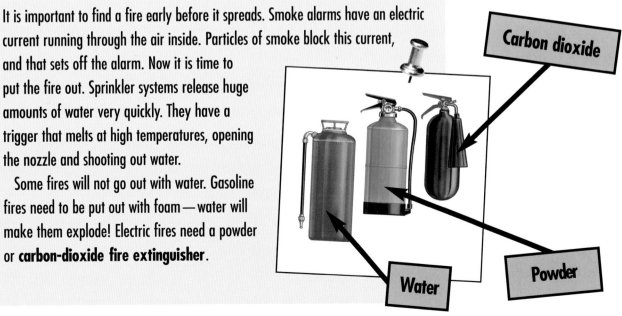

Carbon dioxide

Water

Powder

9

WATER RESCUE

People caught in floods or who have fallen through ice require special help that firefighters can provide. Fire trucks carry floats and diving suits to keep the rescuers warm as they reach survivors in the water. The rescuers are attached at all times to the shore by ropes. Fire hoses are filled with air so that they float and are pushed out across the water for the victims to cling to until help arrives.

THE JAWS OF LIFE

The Jaws of Life are **hydraulic** tools used to cut people from car wrecks. A liquid is pumped into the tool to move its powerful jaws. They can cut right through metal without causing sparks and starting a fuel fire.

Firefighters wrap plane-crash survivors in foil blankets. Although it is thin, the mirror-like material reflects heat back into the body, keeping the person warm.

A rescue team practice saving people from fast-flowing rivers. The rescuers are joined to the water's edge by a rope as they form a human chain out into the middle of the river.

EARTHQUAKE RESCUE

Earthquakes can knock down buildings and trap people inside. This makes rescues difficult, so the latest technology is used to find survivors. **Thermal**-imaging cameras (above) detect a person's body heat beneath mounds of concrete and show rescuers where to dig.

LOOKING FOR CLUES

Firefighters make a note of the smells of a fire, and the colors of the smoke and flames. For example, a fire that burns with yellow-white flames and black smoke might contain gasoline. These facts tell them whether an **accelerant** was used to make the fire burn more rapidly.

11

COAST GUARD

Trusted with keeping American waters safe, the United States Coast Guard helps people and the environment.

The United States Coast Guard has many jobs: a military force that defends the country, a police service that patrols our coasts, and a search-and-rescue team to help people lost at sea. It regulates shipping, prevents smuggling, and responds to oil spills and other **environmental** threats.

The U.S. Coast Guard is in charge of the 200 miles (320 km) of ocean that stretch from the coast. To cover this large area requires ships and other special equipment.

A Coast Guard powerboat is used for rescuing people close to the shore.

KNOW WHERE TO LOOK

Distress beacons on boats and planes help air and sea rescue teams find people lost at sea. Thanks to these beacons, 90 percent of the U.S. Coast Guard's operations are successful rescues. Helicopters and ships know where to look and do not waste time and fuel searching the open ocean.

RESCUE FLEET

The United States Coast Guard is the seventh largest navy in the world, with 39,000 active members.

PIRATE POLICE

The U.S. Coast Guard dates back to 1790. The United States Congress decided to create a force of ten ships to make sure that cargo ships used the **official** ports—and paid taxes when they arrived. At the time, pirates were also a very big problem. That is why the Coast Guard was set up as a military service as well.

Lifeboats are almost unsinkable. They even roll the right way up again after turning over.

A U.S. Coast Guard cutter approaches a sinking cargo ship off an Alaskan coast. The cutter has a helicopter, a crew of 167, and a top speed of 33 miles per hour (54 km/h).

BREAKING THE ICE UP NORTH

Canada has a Coast Guard as well. The Canadian Coast Guard has 18 icebreakers. These are ships with thick bodies and rounded fronts, which ride up on top of sea ice. The ice breaks under the weight of the ship. These ships patrol the Northwest Passage, and keep shipping lanes open. They also respond to distress calls from other ships trapped in ice.

UNSINKABLE

Modern lifeboats are almost unsinkable. They will even roll the right way up again after **capsizing**! The crew is safe in the watertight bridge (control room). Water is pumped into tanks, which makes the boat roll the right way up.

Bridge

Engine

SUBMARINE RESCUE

NATO, an **alliance** between the militaries of Europe and North America, is building a new remote-controlled machine for saving submarine crews. The **submersible** can go nearly 2,000 feet (600 m) down. The vehicle hooks up with a submarine's "rescue seat," the name for the escape hatch. The submarine's crew climbs aboard and is taken to safety.

MODERN FLEET

Today's U.S. Coast Guard's fleet ranges from ocean-going cutters to smaller in-shore lifeboats. Most cutters have landing pads for helicopters. Coast Guard helicopters help in seaching the water for people who need rescuing.

IN THE WATER

Once people in distress are located, rescue teams race to get them out of the water. Heavy waves make it difficult to swim. The water may be so cold that people become unconscious—and there might be sharks. If they had time, the survivors may have put on survival suits. These help them float and keep warm until help arrives.

Helicopters are the best vehicles for a rescue in the ocean. They can go far out to sea more quickly than lifeboats, and they can hover above the decks of sinking ships.

A rescuer is lowered on a **winch** to collect each survivor. Some helicopters drop a rescue swimmer into the ocean. These swimmers brave huge waves and cold water to reach victims. The swimmer puts a survivor in a **harness** or stretcher to be lifted to safety.

> If its engines fail out at sea, a Sea King helicopter can land on water.

EXAMINE THE FACTS

You can compare the work of different coast guards around the world by looking at their websites. There are a few listed below. Do they all do the same things?

www.ccg-gcc.gc.ca
www.mcga.gov.uk
www.uscg.mil

THE SEA KING

The Sea King is one of the most widely used rescue helicopters. The first one was built in 1959. They are still built today because their design is so tough and safe. The Sea King is built to fly far out to sea. It has a winch for lifting people aboard. If the engine fails out at sea, the helicopter can land on water. Floats stored above the wheels **inflate,** keeping the Sea King from sinking.

Diving lifeboats are used on oil and gas platforms, which could explode at any moment after an accident. The lifeboats are built to get into the water—fast! They hit the water with a splash and are ready to motor away within seconds.

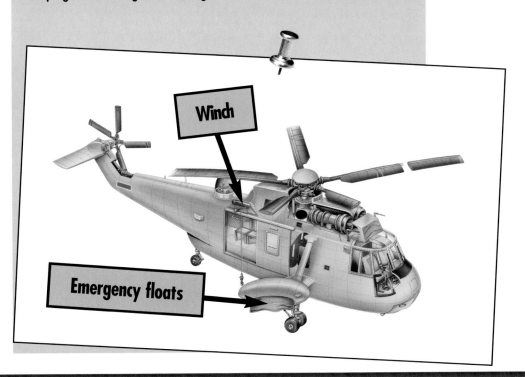

Winch

Emergency floats

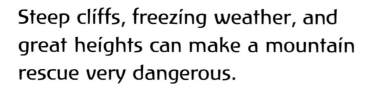

Steep cliffs, freezing weather, and great heights can make a mountain rescue very dangerous.

Mountains attract people with their beauty, their slopes for skiing, and the challenges of climbing them. Climbing to the top can be fun, but mountains are also very dangerous. Rescuers have to be ready when disaster strikes. Special equipment protects mountain rescuers, and helps them to find lost people.

ROCK AND ICE

Mountains collect snow and ice, and they are constantly being **eroded**. Some slopes are at risk of landslides and avalanches. These waves of rock and snow travel down the mountain at great speeds, destroying entire towns, and burying anybody caught in their path.

18

NO-FLY ZONE

The air at the top of the highest mountains is very thin. That makes it impossible for helicopters to fly there. If something goes wrong on these peaks, rescuers can't fly in—they have to climb up.

RESCUE KIT

A mountain rescuer must have the right equipment: waterproof clothing to keep out the cold, ropes, climbing equipment, helmets, and harnesses. Mountain rescuers also have lightweight stretchers to carry victims out of an area.

A mountain rescue team drags an injured person in a sled-stretcher through the snow.

CAVE RESCUE

Mountain rescuers also help people trapped in small spaces like caves. This is a very dangerous type of rescue—it is easy to get trapped yourself. An important job during a cave rescue is keeping track of the equipment and people who enter and leave the cave. That will ensure that no one and nothing is left behind.

RIVERS OF MUD

Volcanoes are the most dangerous mountains. As the forces beneath Earth's surface push the mountain up, eruptions can bring down rivers of **lava**, or even cause parts of the mountain to collapse. A lahar is an **eruption** that melts ice at the top of the mountain. The slush mixes with soil and rocks, producing a mudslide that can demolish towns and drown people. In 1985, a lahar from the Nevado del Ruiz volcano in Columbia killed more than 23,000 people.

HIGH PEAKS

Even if a mountain is not volcanic, there are still many risks for climbers. The air is much thinner at the top of a mountain, and it is much colder. Climbers wear lighweight suits that are waterproof and filled with fluffy material to keep warm. Climbers also carry their own oxygen supplies.

> Rescuers have 15 minutes to dig survivors out of an avalanche. After that, people begin to freeze or suffocate.

Mud and rocks fill a valley after a lahar has run through it from the Tunguragua volcano in Ecuador, South America.

INSIDE AN AVALANCHE

A large avalanche can fill 20 football fields 10 feet (3 m) deep. The snow sets hard and begins to freeze when it stops. People caught in an avalanche must wave their arms to make a breathing space before the snow stops moving. Rescuers (pictured) have about 15 minutes to dig people out. Any longer, and they could begin to freeze or **suffocate**.

SEARCH PATTERNS

To find people who are lost, mountain rescuers must set up a search area. This is a circle drawn around the last place the missing person was known to be. Rescuers then fan out, searching for clues about where the person might have gone. Each new clue adjusts the area where rescuers search.

BE CAREFUL

If you climb a high mountain too fast, your brain can swell in the thin air. This problem is called high-altitude **cerebral edema**, or HACE. People with HACE find it hard to walk and talk, they see things, vomit, go blind, and collapse. But they are also so confused they don't know what is happening. This can make rescues very difficult.

A rescue team practices bringing an injured climber down a **sheer** cliff.

SAVED BY THE PHONE

Sometimes missing people are easy to find—they phone their rescuers! That is what happened when a hiker climbing on Mount Seymore in British Columbia fell more than 300 feet (100 m). His friend called for help on his cell phone. A search-and-rescue team soon arrived. A helicopter was called in and airlifted the injured hiker to safety.

Search-and-rescue teams must work fast and keep in touch with each other.

ON PURPOSE

Sometimes people cause small avalanches to stop a larger one. Experts go up in helicopters and drop explosives on high-risk slopes. This causes a **controlled avalanche**, getting snow out of the way before a dangerous amount builds up.

This method was first used to take lives. During World War I, **Italian** and **Austrian** troops in the Alps would blast mountains to bring avalanches down on their enemies.

Terrorist attacks do not occur very often, but they can threaten many lives at once. Luckily, there are men and women trained to deal with people who want to harm others.

A lot of effort and technology has gone into hunting down terrorists and stopping attacks before they occur. **Counter-terrorism** officers are trained to deal with terrorist threats. They dispose of bombs, spy on people preparing attacks, and even rescue hostages. The skills these officers need and the equipment they use have the same purpose: to rescue people in **hostile** situations and prevent disasters.

ROBOTS

Today, many bomb squads use robots rather than put people in harm's way. These devices can get close to bombs and scan them to detect what type of explosive they are. Experts use that information to decide how to deal with the threat.

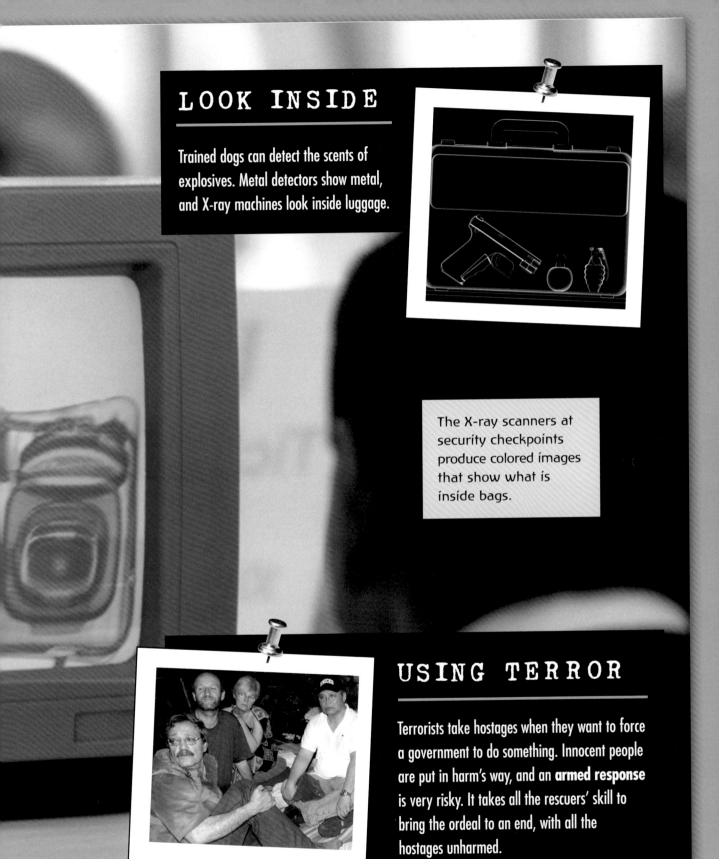

LOOK INSIDE

Trained dogs can detect the scents of explosives. Metal detectors show metal, and X-ray machines look inside luggage.

The X-ray scanners at security checkpoints produce colored images that show what is inside bags.

USING TERROR

Terrorists take hostages when they want to force a government to do something. Innocent people are put in harm's way, and an **armed response** is very risky. It takes all the rescuers' skill to bring the ordeal to an end, with all the hostages unharmed.

BOMB DISPOSAL

In World War I (1914–1918), many **artillery shells** did not work. The British army formed a team of bomb experts to figure out why some explosives failed to go off.

By the 1930s, these same experts were also making unexploded bombs safe. It was risky work. The job got even more dangerous as bombs were designed to be **tamperproof**. Bomb-disposal experts had to find ways of defeating the bombers.

ROBOT DEFENSES

A bomb-disposal robot is sent toward a bomb by remote control. A camera shows what is around the device, and a mechanical arm can break windows, open doors, or even grab the bomb and carry it away. When the package is in a safe place, the armored robot can blow it up without the risk of people being hurt.

A bomb-disposal expert is protected by a blast-proof suit as he demonstrates how a robot can be used.

REAL LIFE

Long after wars have ended, buried **mines** continue to kill or injure 20,000 people each year. Clearing mines is dangerous work—they are designed to explode when touched. A plant is being developed that can detect mines. The flowers of the plant turn red when their roots absorb the gases given off by the explosive in the mines.

A sniffer dog checks a car for a bomb. The dog has been taught to recognize the smell of explosives. If it finds some, it will get a reward from its trainer.

T-ray scanners can look under clothes.

AIRPORT SCANNERS

Many scanners are used in airports. Passengers may have their eyes scanned to check who they are. Before you get on a plane, security will check what you are carrying. They may look inside your bag, but it is harder for them to see what you are carrying under a coat, especially in a crowd.
New T-ray scanners are safer than X rays. They can look under clothes for metals and liquids.

SUITING UP

Bomb-disposal experts are the first line of defense against terrorist bombs. When a bomb is found, bomb-squad members put on heavy blast-proof suits. These suits have metal plates and padding that protect the bomb-disposal expert if the bomb he or she is working on goes off. Some suits even have an air-conditioning unit.

MAKING CONTACT

When terrorists take hostages, the most important person on the rescue team is the hostage **negotiator**. The negotiator works to get the terrorists to let the hostages go, as well as trying to bring an end to the crisis. He or she also encourages the terrorists to get to know their hostages. This can make the terrorists see the hostages as people, making it harder for the terrorists to hurt their prisoners.

Armed police storm a hijacked Cuban airliner at a Florida airport. The hijacker was arrested and all passengers were freed unharmed.

NEGOTIATING

The negotiator tries to bargain with the terrorists, making small deals to keep the hostages safe. Often, the negotiator will offer something to the terrorists in exchange for the release of hostages.

Two negotiators (left and right) talk with some tourists who were taken hostage by terrorists in the Philippines in 2000. The hostages were released unharmed after months of negotiations.

LAST CHANCE

While negotiators are working, the rescue team plans for the worst. If a hostage is harmed, the rescue team may decide to use force to end the crisis. The rescue team learns as much about the area as possible. They need to find out exactly where everyone is. Cameras are lowered down chimneys or fed into air ducts to see what is happening. If the rescue team decides to use force, they move in very quickly and in large numbers. The terrorists must be taken by surprise so they cannot defend themselves or hurt the hostages. Non-lethal weapons, such as knock-out gas or stun grenades, are sometimes used to **incapacitate** the terrorists without harming the hostages.

REAL LIFE

Sometimes, hostages develop what is called Stockholm Syndrome, named after a hostage drama in Stockholm, Sweden. Hostages become friendly with the people that took them and start to agree with their demands. They might not want to escape, even when the opportunity arises. This is another reason why it is very important rescue teams work quickly to free hostages.

GLOSSARY

accelerant A fast-burning fuel that sets fire to everything else around it

alliance A group that has agreed to work together

armed response The use of weapons

artillery shells Explosives fired from large guns used in battles

Austrian A person from Austria, a country in Europe

avalanche When snow slides down the side of a mountain

beacons Warning signals

bunks A narrow shelf-like bed

capsizing A boat turning upside down in the water

carbon dioxide A gas that stops things from burning

cerebral edema When too much water collects in the brain

controlled avalanche A man-made avalanche, used to prevent the potentially dangerous build-up of snow on mountains

counter-terrorism Working against terrorism

detective A person who figures out what happened at the scene of a fire

distress In trouble

emergency services Public organizations that respond to emergencies when they occur. These include police, ambulance, and firefighting services

environmental To do with the health of the environment

eroded Gradually worn away

eruption When gas, smoke, and melted rocks flood out of a volcano

fire extinguisher A hand-held machine used to put out fires

fuel Something that burns easily and is used to provide heat or power an engine

harness Belts and straps that attach a person to a winch

hostages People held prisoner by criminals

hostile Ready to use violence against other people

hydraulic A machine with moving parts that are powered by liquid being pumped through them

incapacitate To make someone unable to move

inflate To fill with air

Italian A person from Italy, a country in Europe

lava Melted rock that flows out of a volcano

mines Bombs that explode when touched or stepped on

negotiator A person whose job it is to make deals

official Something that is real, genuine, and proper

oxygen A gas in the air that helps things burn

sheer A cliff that is so steep that it goes straight up

submersible A small submarine; submersibles generally go deeper than submarines do

suffocate To die after running out of air

tamperproof Designed to be difficult to change or alter

thermal Another word for "heat"

winch A machine that lowers and raises a rope or cable

Books

Avalanche and Landslide Alert! by Amanda Bishop and Vanessa Walker.
New York, NY: Crabtree Publishing, 2005.

Catching Fire: The Story of Firefighting by Gena K. Gorrel. Toronto,
Canada: Tundra Books: 1999.

Firefighting: Behind the Scenes by Maria Mudd-Ruth. Boston,
MA: Houghton Mifflin, 1998.

Machines at Work—Emergency by Ian Graham. Laguna Hills,
CA: QEB Publishing, 2006.

Mountains by Margaret Hynes. Boston, MA: Kingfisher, 2007.

Rescues! by Sandra Markle. Minneapolis, MN: Millbrook Press, 2006.

Websites

Canadian Coast Guard Icebreaking Program:
http://www.ccg-gcc.gc.ca/eng/CCG/Icebreaking

Hazard House Fire Safety World:
http://www.hazardhouse.com/denverfirefightersmuseum

International Spy Museum:
http://www.spymuseum.org/operationspy/index.php

Royal National Lifeboat Institution, Shore Thing:
http://www.rnli.org.uk/Shorething/Youth/Default.aspx

A

accelerants 11
avalanches 4, 5, 18,
  21, 23

B

beacons, distress 13
blankets, foil 10
bomb detection
  and disposal
  4, 24, 26, 27
bunker gear 8–9

C

Canadian Coast Guard
  14
car accidents 7, 10
carbon dioxide 9
cave rescue 20
cell phones 23
Coast Guards 4, 5,
  12–17
counter-terrorism 24
cutters (ships) 14, 15

D

dogs 5, 25, 27

E

earthquake rescue 11
emergency services 4, 5

F

fire extinguishers 9
firefighters 4, 5, 6–11
forest fires 8

H

HACE 22
helicopters 4, 8, 13, 14,
  15, 16, 17, 19, 23
hijackers 28
hostages 5, 24, 25,
  28–29

I

icebreakers 14

J

Jaws of Life 10

L

lahars 20, 21
lifeboats 14, 15, 16, 17

M

metal detectors 25
mines 26
mountain rescue 5, 18–23

N

NATO 15
negotiators, hostage 28–29

P

pirates 14
plane crashes 10
police officers 5, 12, 28

R

rivers, rescue from
  6, 11
robots, bomb-disposal
  24, 26

S

Sea King 16, 17
search and rescue 12, 23
smoke alarms 9
sprinkler systems 9
Stockholm Syndrome 29
submarine 15
survival suits 16

T

terrorist threat 4, 24–29
thermal-imaging equipment
  11
T-ray scanners 27

V

volcanoes 20, 21

X

X-ray scanners 25, 27

Printed in the U.S.A.